At the Top of Their Game

I0884502

Lionel Messi

Legendary Soccer Player

Kate Shoup

Cavendish Square
New York

Published in 2020 by Cavendish Square Publishing, LLC
243 5th Avenue, Suite 136, New York, NY 10016

First Edition

Library of Congress Cataloging-in-Publication Data

Names: Shoup, Kate, 1972- author.
Title: Lionel Messi : legendary soccer player / Kate Shoup.
Description: First edition. | New York : Cavendish Square, 2020. | Series: At the top of their game | Audience: Grades: 9 to 12. | Includes bibliographical references and index.
Identifiers: LCCN 2019015710 (print) | LCCN 2019019517 (ebook) | ISBN 9781502651198 (ebook) | ISBN 9781502651181 (library bound) | ISBN 9781502651167 (pbk.) | ISBN 9781502651174 (6 pack)
Subjects: LCSH: Messi, Lionel, 1987- –Juvenile literature. | Soccer players–Argentina–Biography–Juvenile literature.
Classification: LCC GV942.7.M398 (ebook) | LCC GV942.7.M398 S56 2020 (print) | DDC 796.334092 [B] –dc23
LC record available at https://lccn.loc.gov/2019015710

Editor: Jodyanne Benson
Copy Editor: Michele Suchomel-Casey
Associate Art Director: Alan Sliwinski
Designer: Joe Parenteau
Production Coordinator: Karol Szymczuk
Photo Research: J8 Media

The photographs in this book are used by permission and through the courtesy of: Cover, p. 64 VI-Images/Getty Images; p. 4 Natursports/Shutterstock.com; pp. 7, 54 Maxisport/Shutterstock.com; pp. 10, 26-27 ZUMA Press, Inc./Alamy Stock Photo; pp. 12-13 Xinhua/Alamy Stock Photo; p. 17 ESB Professional/Shutterstock.com; p. 22 Bob Thomas/Bob Thomas Sports Photography/Getty Images; p. 28 Josep Lago/AFP/Getty Images; p. 31 Julian Finney-FIFA/Getty Images; pp. 34-35 Hector Rio/AFP/Getty Images; pp. 38-39 CosminIftode/Shutterstock.com; p. 40 Carlos Carrion/AFP/Getty Images; p. 42 El Grafico/Getty Images; pp. 46-47 Jordiferrer/Wikimedia Commons/File:Ciutat Esportiva Joan Gamper-2.JPG/CC BY-SA 3.0; p. 49 charnsitr/Shutterstock.com; p. 56 Clive Mason/Getty Images; p. 59 Lars Baron/Bongarts/Getty Images; p. 60 Miguel Ruiz/FC Barcelona/Getty Images; pp. 66-67 Ververidis Vasilis/Shutterstock.com; p. 69 Manuel Queimadelos Alonso/Getty Images; pp. 76-77 Shaun Botterill-FIFA/Getty Images; pp. 80-81 Catherine Ivill/Getty Images; p. 84 Miquel Benitez/WireImage/Getty Images; p. 90 Power Sport Images/Getty Images; pp. 92-93 basiczto/Shutterstock.com; p. 95 Karim Jaafar/AFP/Getty Images.

Printed in the United States of America

At the Top of Their Game

Contents

Qatar
Foundation
LFP

Introduction

The Best in History

When Lionel Messi was born on June 24, 1987, in Rosario, Argentina, his parents never imagined he would become one of the best soccer players—if not *the* best—in history. However, that's exactly what happened! From a very early age, Lionel was a natural when it came to soccer.

A Gifted Player

Lionel's family discovered his gift for playing soccer when he was just four years old. Lionel's grandmother arranged for him to play for a nearby club called Grandoli. He switched to a different club called Newell's Old Boys when he was six years old.

Lionel played for Newell's with the same core group of boys for six years. Together they won nearly every match they played. Lionel was the team's top scorer. He averaged around one hundred goals per season. He drove the other teams crazy.

Opposite: Lionel Messi is one of the best soccer players of all time.

La Pulga

Lionel was very small for his age. His brothers and teammates called him *la pulga* (the flea). When he was nine years old, he stopped growing completely. He stood just 4 feet 2 inches (1.3 meters) tall, which was 4 inches (10 centimeters) shorter than an average boy his age. A doctor discovered that Lionel suffered from a growth hormone deficiency.

Lionel was lucky. His condition could be treated with a daily injection of growth hormone. However, his treatment was expensive. His parents couldn't pay. Newell's helped cover the cost for a while but stopped. Lionel's parents became desperate.

FC Barcelona

Soon, a solution presented itself. A famous soccer club called Fútbol Club (FC) Barcelona in Spain found out about Lionel. The team flew Lionel and his father to Barcelona for a tryout. They were impressed with what they saw. They offered Lionel a spot at the club's youth academy. They also agreed to pay for his treatment. When Lionel was thirteen years old, he moved to Spain.

On the pitch (another name for a soccer field) Lionel excelled. He impressed all his coaches. Even the other players could see how talented he was.

Off the pitch, however, he struggled. He was very homesick. Even though his father had moved to Spain with him, his mother and siblings were

When Lionel Messi first moved to Barcelona, he struggled, but eventually he found his footing!

back home in Rosario. Lionel was also very shy. He had trouble making friends. Eventually, Lionel settled in. He made friends and became less homesick. Having reached a normal adult height of 5 feet 7 inches (1.7 m), Lionel also completed his course of medical treatment.

Lionel quickly moved up in the ranks at the youth academy. He played his first official match with FC Barcelona's top team in October of 2004. He was seventeen years old.

By the 2005–2006 season, Lionel was a full-time member of the main squad. By the 2006–2007, season he was a starter. He quickly became a fan favorite. In addition to playing for FC Barcelona, Lionel also joined Argentina's junior national team and later the senior squad.

Finding Success

Lionel Messi really broke out in the 2008–2009 season. That year, he led FC Barcelona to a record-breaking six championships and won a gold medal with Argentina at the Olympics held in Beijing, China. In 2018, Messi became the team captain of FC Barcelona.

Messi has earned hundreds of millions of dollars and an impressive number of awards playing soccer. He was the highest paid athlete in the world in 2019. During his career with FC Barcelona, Messi has won nine Spanish league crowns, four European league titles, and nineteen other major cups or championships as of 2019. He has also set several records. For example, he is the all-time top scorer in both the Spanish and European leagues.

Messi has been less successful with Argentina's national team, however. Although he led the team to victory in the U-20 World Cup in 2005, a senior World Cup title has eluded him as of 2019.

Off the pitch, Messi loves spending time with his family. In 2017, Messi married his childhood sweetheart. Her name is Antonella Roccuzzo. The couple have three sons: Thiago, Mateo, and Ciro.

When he isn't scoring on the pitch, Messi also does lots of charity work. "I always dreamed of succeeding at what I loved best, which was football, and being able to make a career out of it," Messi has said. "I've had to face many hurdles along the way, and it was tough, but I never stopped dreaming about what I wanted, and fortunately I've been able to fulfill those dreams." This book tells the story of how Lionel Messi achieved his dreams both on and off the pitch.

Chapter 1
The Early Years

Lionel Andrés Messi was born on June 24, 1987. He was named after a famous singer: Lionel Richie. His parents called him Leo for short. He came from humble roots, and his humility is something that people notice when he plays soccer. He holds his teammates in very high regard, and he is motivated by his love for the game.

Humble Roots

Lionel's mother, Celia, worked at a magnet factory and later became a cleaner. His father, Jorge, was a supervisor at a steel plant. They were married in 1978. Lionel has two older brothers. His oldest brother, Rodrigo, was born in 1980. Next came Matías. He was born in 1982. A younger sister named María Sol arrived in 1993.

The Messi family lived in Rosario, Argentina. Argentina is in South America. Rosario is the third most populous city in Argentina. It's an industrial city, which means it has lots of factories. It is about

Opposite: A young Lionel Messi is shown here kneeling (*second from right*) in a team photograph that hangs on the wall of the Grandoli Football Club.

Fans of Messi often visit his childhood home in Rosario, Argentina.

TAXI

185 miles (298 kilometers) inland from Buenos Aires. Buenos Aires is the country's capital.

The Messi family didn't have a lot of money. They had what they needed to get by. They lived in a two-story brick house in the Las Heras neighborhood. It could be a rough neighborhood at times, but it was not a slum. Lionel's father and grandfather built the house with their own hands. The house had a backyard where Lionel and his brothers and sister could play. Lionel's grandparents lived around the corner. His cousins Emanuel and Maximiliano also lived nearby. Lionel was close with them.

Life in Argentina

Like many Argentines, the Messi family did their best to cope with political instability and a tough economy. The main reason for the country's political upheaval was a coup d'état that occurred in 1976. The military replaced President Isabel Perón with a career officer named Jorge Rafael Videla. Videla ruled as a dictator. He suspended Congress. He closed the courts. He outlawed political parties and banned labor unions. Military officials filled all key government posts. Videla ordered the murder of anyone who spoke out against him. More than thirty thousand Argentines "disappeared." This meant that they were kidnapped, tortured, and murdered. Their bodies were never found.

Under Videla, the country's economy crumbled. It went into a recession. People lost their jobs. At the same time, prices rose. This made it even harder for people to afford basic goods. (This is called inflation.) This period was particularly difficult for middle-class families like the Messi family. By 1983, the Argentine people had had enough. They were tired of living in a poor economy. They also saw the military government as corrupt and resented its violent practices. They were also angry because the Argentine military had started a war against Great Britain over who owned a series of islands called the Falkland Islands. Argentina lost the war.

In October of 1983, the Argentine people pushed out the military dictatorship and elected new leaders. The chaos wasn't quite over, however. In 1986 and 1987, the military pressured the Argentine government to pass two laws. These laws prevented soldiers who had murdered civilians during the military dictatorship from being punished. Many Argentines were upset by these laws—especially those who had lost loved ones under the military dictatorship. Around the same time, the government announced higher prices for basic things like milk, eggs, sugar, corn, electricity, and gas. These price increases hit middle-class families like the Messi family hard.

On the day Lionel was born, protestors set off fifteen bombs throughout Argentina. One of these was in Lionel's hometown of Rosario. Another was in nearby Villa Constitución. No one was killed or injured, but the bombs showed how divided the country was. Some thought it might be on the brink of civil war. Fortunately, things calmed down after that.

Soccer in Argentina

During the military dictatorship, many Argentines turned to soccer (also called football) as a form of escape—including the Messi family. "We have always loved football in our family," said Lionel's mother. Soccer is a ball game played by two teams with eleven players each. They play on a large rectangular field called a pitch with a goal on each end. The object of the game is to put the ball in the other team's goal. The team that scores the most goals wins; however, depending on the format, a draw or tie may be allowed. Except for the goalkeeper, whose job is to protect his or her team's goal, players may not use their hands or arms to move the ball. Instead, they move the ball by kicking it with their feet. They can also use their legs, knees, chest, or head to move the ball.

"People have enjoyed kicking a ball about for thousands of years," said the Fédération Internationale de Football Association (FIFA). FIFA is the sport's international governing body. Modern soccer evolved from another popular sport called rugby football. In 1863, representatives from several sports clubs in London met to define the rules of soccer. They also created a new organization to govern the game in England. It was called the Football Association (FA). The sport became known as association football or just football. Only people in the United States and a few other countries call it soccer. According to the *Oxford English Dictionary*, the word "soccer" is an abbreviation of the word "association" plus the suffix "-er."

Soccer quickly grew in popularity. By 1871, fifty teams had joined the FA. The FA organized the world's first-ever knockout soccer tournament in 1872. In a knockout tournament, the loser of each match is eliminated from the tournament, and the winner advances to the next round. If both teams score the same number of goals, the match goes into extra time or a shootout. In 1888, it launched a league championship.

British players who moved abroad brought soccer with them. British railroad workers in Buenos Aires brought soccer to Argentina. The first match occurred there in June 1867. In 1893, the Argentine Football Association (AFA) was formed. The AFA is one of the sport's oldest national governing bodies. It was the first governing body formed outside the United Kingdom. Today, soccer is by far the most popular sport in Argentina.

In 1978, during the height of the military dictatorship, Argentina hosted the World Cup tournament. This tournament has been played every four years since 1930. (Play was cancelled in 1942 and 1946 due to World War II.) It's the most famous and important soccer tournament in the world. Argentina not only hosted the 1978 World Cup, but it also won the tournament. This victory united the nation in glory but also provided cover for the violent Videla regime by distracting the Argentine people.

Lionel received his first soccer ball—a white ball with red diamonds—at the age of four.

Lionel's First Ball

One day, Lionel's father and brothers were kicking a soccer ball around in the street in front of the family home. Four-year-old Lionel decided to join in. This was a first. Lionel's parents had given him a white soccer ball with red diamonds for his fourth birthday, but so far, no one had seen him play. It turned out Lionel was quite a gifted player. His family was stunned by what he could do.

It wasn't just that Lionel had a natural talent for soccer. He also loved the game. He used to kick the ball around continuously—sometimes with his brothers or cousins but usually by himself. He used to drive his neighbors crazy kicking the ball against the wall outside his house. A neighbor confirms this. "He was a quiet child," the family's next-door neighbor said. "My only problem with him was that he used to interrupt my siesta—all the time kicking a football against a wall."

Lionel remembers this as well. "As a child I always had a ball on me, from the time I woke up to the moment I went to bed. More than once I slept with my ball," said Lionel. He often played with his friends in the streets even after it got dark. "Those moments with my friends and the ball—just us, no coaches—are beautiful memories for me," he explained. He would continue to use that passion for soccer as motivation throughout his career.

Joining the Squad at Grandoli

Lionel's brothers Rodrigo and Matías played on a soccer team at Grandoli Football Club. It was a small pitch with patchy grass in a rough part of town. Rodrigo played the center-forward position.

Coaches described him as speedy and powerful. Matías was a defender.

Some parents push their kids to play sports—not Celia and Jorge. It was Lionel's grandmother (also named Celia) who encouraged the Messi boys to play soccer and who took Rodrigo and Matías to practice at Grandoli. Lionel was too young to play, but he often tagged along.

One day in 1991, a coach at the club named Salvador Aparico was short one player for the '86 team. This team consisted of players born in 1986—one year before Lionel. Aparico spotted a little boy kicking a ball around. That boy was Lionel. Aparico asked Lionel's grandmother if she would lend the boy to him. Celia readily agreed. She knew how talented Lionel was. "Put him on," she told Aparico. So, he did.

Early in the game, the ball rolled to Lionel. He didn't move. He just looked at it. Aparico was unimpressed. The next time the ball rolled to Lionel, however, he took control. He dribbled it down the pitch, past all the other players, to the goal. Lionel didn't score, but he proved to Aparico that he had real talent. Lionel played on Aparico's team for the rest of the season.

Before long, he was scoring half a dozen goals per match—and sometimes more. "He was born knowing how to play," Aparico said of Lionel. Grandoli Football Club's current president, David Treves, agreed. "He had something since he was born. It was stunning what they saw him do at the age of four. He was doing the kinds of things that he does today but then the ball came up to his knees," said Treves. The next year, Lionel's dad, Jorge, took over as coach. The team won everything—every friendly game, every tournament, and the championship. Lionel began attracting lots of local attention.

When Lionel played, the whole neighborhood came out to watch—even people who weren't connected to the club.

Lionel's abilities were even more remarkable considering his size. He was very small—much smaller than his teammates and rivals. In one early team photo, Lionel's white pants are so big they practically reach his armpits, and he appears to be drowning in his jersey.

Maradona and Messi

Lionel continued to leave an impression. "We were worried how [Lionel] would progress considering his lack of growth. But his technical skills made us think we were looking at the next [Diego] Maradona," said Treves. To be called "the next Maradona" is a big compliment. Diego Maradona is a famous Argentine soccer player who "had that magic, that special something that makes you realize you're dealing with something out of this world, the likes of which will never be seen again," explained Italian writer Luciano Crescenzo. Another Argentine soccer player named Carlos Tevez observed, "Diego, for all Argentinians, is God. And he always will be."

It's true that Messi and Maradona are similar in many ways—despite their twenty-seven-year difference in age. Both are from Argentina. Both showed amazing promise from a young age, and both went on to have amazing careers on the pitch. Both are also on the small side. (Maradona is even shorter than Messi.) Both are left-footed. Both have similar playing styles. "From an extraordinarily early age, there was a sense that Maradona was somehow marked for greatness, special," said author Jonathan Wilson. The same was true for Lionel Messi.

However, there are differences, too. For example, their personalities are completely opposite. Jeff Himmelman of the *New York Times* described Maradona as "larger than life," observing that he "loves to party, got heavily into drugs, makes questionable decisions and is always boiling over about something and making headlines." In contrast, Messi is shy and reserved.

Another difference is that Messi grew up in a middle-class family, whereas Maradona's was very poor. He lived with his parents and seven siblings in a slum on the outskirts of Buenos Aires. The family's house was nothing more than a tiny shack built from loose bricks and sheets of metal. It had no electricity or running water. Often, it fell to Diego to make extra money for the family. He did whatever odd job he could find. He opened taxi doors for tips and scavenged for discarded cigarette packets to sell the aluminum foil wrapping for scrap.

When Diego was three years old, his cousin gave him a soccer ball. He played with it constantly—kicking it against a wire fence near his family's shack until he dented it. When the ball wasn't around, he made do with other objects. He practiced keepie-uppies with whatever he could find. (Keepie-uppies is also called juggling. It involves using one's feet, knees, legs, chest, shoulders, or head to keep a ball or other object from touching the ground.) Sometimes he played with an orange or a wadded-up newspaper—even a bundle of rags.

When Diego was eight years old, he tried out for a team called Los Cebollitas (the Little Onions). It was the youth squad for the Argentinos Juniors professional ("pro") team. "I was struck by his talent and couldn't believe he was only eight years old," said Los Cebollitas coach Francisco Cornejo of Maradona. Cornejo even asked Diego to produce his ID (identification) card so they could

To many, Diego Maradona is the greatest soccer player of all time.

verify his age. "We were sure he was having us on because, although he had the physique of a child, he played like an adult." Diego made the team. He would go on to guide Los Cebollitas to 140 straight wins and a national junior championship in 1972.

Diego often performed tricks with a soccer ball during halftime at Argentinos Juniors matches to entertain the crowd. This drew the attention of a newspaper reporter when Diego was ten years old. "He is left-footed but knows how to use the right" and displayed a "rare ability to control and dribble with the ball," wrote the reporter. "He can kill the ball, and then just as easily lift it up with both his feet. He holds himself like a born football player." Coaches promoted Diego to the Argentinos Juniors pro team in 1976. He was just sixteen years old. Diego became known as *El Pibe de Oro* (the Golden Boy).

Over the next twenty-one years, Maradona would play for professional clubs in Argentina, Spain, and Italy. These included Argentinos Juniors, Boca Juniors, Fútbol Club Barcelona (like Messi), SSC Napoli, Società Sportiva Calcio Napoli, Sevilla Fútbol Club, and Newell's Old Boys (again, like Messi). In club play, Maradona competed in 490 matches and scored 259 goals. Maradona also played 91 games and scored 34 goals for Argentina's national squad. Led by Diego Maradona, that squad won the World Cup in 1986, which was one year before Lionel Messi was born.

Maradona retired in 1997. In 2000, FIFA named Maradona the Player of the Century—an award he shared with a Brazilian named Edson Arantes do Nascimento (known as Pelé). Pelé is regarded by many in the sport as one of the greatest players in history.

Lionel Messi will also leave a great soccer legacy. However, because he is still playing, it will be some time before we know exactly what that legacy is.

Early Idols

Lionel Messi was no doubt thrilled to be compared to Maradona. Like most Argentines, young Lionel idolized Maradona. "Of course I admired Maradona," Lionel later told a reporter. "He was a real inspiration for me." However, he wasn't Lionel's only role model.

Another idol of Lionel's was a young Argentine midfielder named Pablo Aimar. "When Pablo Aimar started to break through, I used to really enjoy watching him play," Lionel said. Aimar was eight years older than Lionel. He became a professional player in 1996 at age seventeen for a team called River Plate in Buenos Aires. Later, he played in Spain. Some called Aimar "the wizard," said journalist Paul Wilson. Others called him "the clown (because he entertained with his tricks)." Most hailed him as "some kind of football genius ... [with] delicate but quite definite gifts of touch, control and vision." Aimar was described as "the new Maradona," just like Messi would be. Maradona himself once called Aimar "the only player I would pay to watch" and referred to him as "my natural heir."

Lionel also admired the Brazilian player Cristiano Ronaldo. "Ronaldo was my hero," Lionel once told a reporter. "He was the best forward I've ever seen. He was so fast that he could score a goal from nothing and he struck the ball better than anyone I've seen." Ronaldo is still a popular professional player today.

Moving to Newell's Old Boys

At the age of six, Lionel was recruited to play for another club in his hometown of Rosario called Newell's Old Boys. Newell's Old Boys was founded in 1903. The club fielded several soccer teams. These ranged from squads for young players like Lionel to a professional team that played in Argentina's top league. This league used to be called the Primera División. Now, it's called the Superliga Argentina.

Other teams in the Superliga Argentina include Rosario Central, Argentinos Juniors, Boca Juniors, River Plate, and others. Coincidentally, Maradona played for the Newell's Old Boys professional squad during the 1993–1994 season. Young Lionel was in the stands for Maradona's debut with the team.

It was as if Lionel was destined to play for Newell's. He had even received a red-and-black Newell's jersey for his first birthday—a gift from his aunts and uncles. His father Jorge, his brothers Rodrigo and Matías, and his cousins Emanuel and Maximiliano had also played for the team.

When Lionel first arrived at Newell's, his coaches had doubts about him. "When you saw him you would think: this kid can't play ball. He's … too fragile, too small," said one coach, Adrián Coria. Lionel quickly proved them wrong. In his first match with the club, he scored an impressive four goals. He would score hundreds more in the next six years.

The stadium at Newell's Old Boys in Rosario, Argentina, was also home to Diego Maradona. Messi played for the Old Boys youth squad from the time he was six until he was thirteen.

A. MARADONA
LA HINCHADA MAS
irb.com
VISA
HARD
FIELD

uhlsport
inter
apuestas
.com
LFP
unicef
NICO PAREJA
16

Chapter

2

Rising Star

At Newell's Old Boys, Lionel Messi was part of a team of players born the same year he was (1987). The squad was so successful that it became known as La Maquina del '87 (The '87 Machine). Lionel emerged as one of the most phenomenal players his coaches had ever seen.

Success with the Machine

At first, La Maquina played a type of soccer called baby football. This game has seven players per team and is played on a smaller pitch. Lionel's baby football squad was unbeatable. In three years, the squad never lost a game. The same was true when the group graduated to the normal eleven-player-per-side format. The team won tournaments all over Argentina and even as far away as Brazil. This thrilled everyone on the team but the goalkeeper—who sometimes grew "so bored during the beatings his outfield teammates were administering, he would sit on his backside in the box," said soccer journalist Richard Fitzpatrick.

Opposite: Lionel Messi battles for the ball in a 2008 match against RCD Espanyol.

Lionel was the team's "engine," said Messi biographer Messinardo Faccio. He averaged around one hundred goals per season. Lionel's coach Adrián Coria described him as explosive and dominating. One-on-one, the other players didn't stand a chance. Lionel destroyed his defenders, anticipating their every step and constantly catching them wrong-footed. His ball control was incredible—it was as if the ball was tethered to his foot.

Lionel was small—just 3 feet 11 inches (1.2 meters) tall. Now, it wasn't just his brothers who called him la pulga (the flea); to Lionel's dismay, his teammates did, too. However, it didn't matter. The bigger boys lacked Lionel's coordination and ability to control the ball. Lionel left them in the dust. Diego Maradona became familiar with Lionel during this period. "Even though the ball was bigger than him, he was never afraid. He never cried. He played better when they kicked him. He was always brave. He wanted to play with the ball, to dribble, to go forward," Maradona said of young Messi. Lionel stood out from the rest with his natural gift of playing soccer.

Lionel drove other teams mad. During one match, he did five "sombreros" on the boy guarding him. (A sombrero is when a player steps over the ball and uses his or her heel to flick it off the ground from behind so that the ball arcs forward over the opponent's head.) Another time, Lionel nutmegged an opponent twice in one play. (Nutmegging is when a player kicks the ball through an opponent's legs.)

To motivate Lionel, one of his early coaches, Carlos Marconi, promised him a special Argentine chocolate cookie called an *alfajores* for each goal. There was just one problem: More often than not, Lionel scored four or five goals per game. Marconi needed to up the ante. To make things harder, he promised Lionel two alfajores

Adrián Coria coached Messi at Newell's Old Boys.

per goal—*if* Messi scored the goal using his head. "The next game, Messi dribbled through the entire opposing team, including the goalkeeper, then stopped at the goal line to flick the ball up into the air with his foot so that he could head it into the empty net," said Jeff Himmelman of the *New York Times*. "When he found Marconi's eye in the stands, Messi smiled and held up two fingers." Marconi knew Lionel was something special.

A Desire to Win

Lionel was competitive. He liked to win, but that wasn't all. For example, if the team won a game, but Lionel failed to score, he got angry. That was just his personality.

Even though Lionel was consistently the best kid on the field, he worked constantly to improve. A teammate on La Maquina named Bruno Milanesio said, "Every day, he trained to be better. He always wanted more, more, more. He put football above everything." To this day, Messi is motivated by his passion for the game.

Lionel was intense, but he wasn't full of himself. Despite his obvious talent, he was quite humble. He also looked out for others. Ernesto Vecchio, one of Lionel's coaches, observed this quality: "I remember one time he received the ball from his own goalkeeper and just started going past each member of the opposing team, eliminating them one by one until he reached the rival keeper." When Lionel darted past, the keeper hurt his leg. "Messi, instead of kicking the ball into an empty net, stopped and asked the ref to get medical attention for the keeper," said Vecchio. Lionel's humility on the pitch is very much admired by his fans.

In addition to being humble, Lionel was also quite shy (painfully so)—that is, until you got to know him. He might stay silent around

Adrián Coria

Adrián Coria worked at Newell's Old Boys. He coached the La Maquina del '87 squad from the time Lionel was eleven to the time he was thirteen.

After Lionel left for Barcelona, Coria worked as a coach for the Paraguayan national team. He was the head coach of the Paraguayan youth national team called the under-twenty (U-20) squad. He also worked as an assistant coach on the Paraguayan senior national team. His boss was named Gerardo "Tata" Martino.

In 2013, FC Barcelona hired Martino as its head coach. Martino brought his assistant Coria with him. After thirteen years apart, Coria and Messi were reunited. (Lionel was also close with Martino before his arrival at Barcelona.)

Coria is widely credited with "discovering" Lionel Messi. He pushed hard for Newell's to help pay for Lionel's medical treatment for his growth hormone disorder (GHD). When the team failed to do so, Coria was upset. "They didn't want to spend money on a thirteen-year-old kid," Coria said. "I think they didn't realize the value of what was right in front of them," he said. Little did they know, Lionel would go on to become a legendary soccer star.

Messi attended the General Las Heras school in Rosario, Argentina. Today, a mural of Messi appears on the school's outer wall.

10
messi

people he doesn't know. However, "when he is with his mates," said Maradona, "he's great fun ... I remember him as a funny guy, entertaining, extroverted but also a very respectful person, modest, unassuming." These qualities would end up serving Messi well when he eventually became a team captain for his Barcelona team.

Trouble at School

Lionel might have been a star on the soccer pitch, but he struggled at school. He just wasn't a good student. In particular, he had trouble reading; however, he eventually improved. During classroom time, Lionel sat quietly. He rarely spoke.

Recess was another story. When Lionel went outside for playtime, he blossomed. He would gather a group of children for a quick game of soccer—dazzling even the older ones with his amazing abilities. "He felt more at ease on the pitch than in the classroom," recalled one of his teachers, named Diana Ferrato. Lionel dominated the other kids on the pitch at school, but he never bragged. He was modest. "I never heard him boast about playing well and scoring goals," said another teacher, Mónica Dómina. Modesty, humility, intensity, and competitiveness are all qualities that have helped Messi become both a star player and role model.

A Sad Loss

In 1998, when Lionel was ten years old, his grandmother Celia died. She was sixty-eight years old. Lionel was deeply saddened by his grandmother's death. He never forgot that it was Celia who had encouraged him to play football and who had convinced Coach Aparico at Grandoli Football Club to put him on the pitch for the very first time. Celia had also been the one to persuade Lionel's parents to buy him his first pair of soccer shoes.

Today, Messi often celebrates goals by looking up and pointing at the sky. This is to honor his grandmother Celia. "I think about her a lot," Messi said. "I would have loved that she was here in the stadium, watching me, enjoying it. She gave us everything … I dedicate my goals and my triumphs to her." In this way, Celia remains in Messi's heart through each game.

The Smallest Kid on the Field

Lionel was always small. That's why people called him la pulga (the flea). By the time he was nine and a half, he stood just 4 feet 2 inches (1.27 m) tall and had stopped growing completely. He was 4 inches (10 cm) shorter than the average boy his age. Clearly there was a problem. Lionel's coaches at Newell's arranged for the boy to see an endocrinologist. An endocrinologist is a doctor who specializes in health issues related to hormones. Hormones are chemicals in the body that control certain bodily functions such as growth.

The doctor's name was Dr. Diego Schwarzstein. "A man from the club told me that they had a kid who was brilliant but very, very small," Dr. Schwarzstein recalled. "They wanted me to see if I could help him grow." Dr. Schwarzstein concluded that Lionel suffered from a condition called growth hormone disorder (GHD). This disorder prevented Lionel's body from producing enough of the hormones needed to grow. The type of GHD Lionel had afflicts about one in every twenty thousand people.

The good news was that Lionel's condition was treatable. His treatment involved a daily injection of growth hormones. Lionel administered this shot himself. It was a relatively painless procedure—"less noticeable than a mosquito bite," said journalist Richard Fitzgerald. Lionel took it in stride. Dr. Schwarzstein commented, "He dealt with all the tests … and the therapy, without too much trouble." He was impressed by Lionel's resilience and perseverance.

Financial Woes

Lionel's medical treatment was very expensive—about 40,000 Argentine pesos ($1,000) per month. At first, this wasn't a problem because people who lived in Argentina were eligible for health insurance through a government program. The government program paid for the medical treatments.

However, in 1998, Argentina entered an economic depression that was brought about by failures in government policy. This meant that 20 percent of Argentines were completely out of work.

Messi often looks up and points to the sky after scoring a goal. This is to honor his grandmother Celia, who died when Messi was ten.

Dr. Diego Schwarzstein treated Messi for growth hormone disorder (GHD).

Even those Argentines who happened to be lucky enough to keep their jobs found that their wages didn't stretch as far as they used to because of an 18 percent average decrease in their pay.

More than 50 percent of Argentines were also living below the poverty line. Of these, half were indigent. This meant even their most basic needs went unmet.

Fortunately, Jorge and Celia were able to keep their jobs. However, the country's insurance program lost funding. It could no longer pay for Lionel's care. Now, it fell to Jorge and Celia to cover the bill for his treatments—something they just couldn't afford.

At the urging of Coach Adrián Coria, Newell's Old Boys stepped in to help. The club offered to cover every other injection. Soon, though, the payments began to arrive late, and then they stopped arriving completely. Lionel's parents grew frustrated.

Jorge approached another club, River Plate in Buenos Aires, for help. The club showed interest—Lionel even tried out for the team—but the deal never materialized. Lionel's parents became desperate. They needed some way to pay for his treatment. Fortunately, a solution was about to present itself.

Chapter 3

Barcelona Bound

Lionel Messi was thirteen years old. He still needed two years of expensive treatment to ensure he grew to a normal size. Despite his obvious talent, no soccer clubs in his native Argentina were willing to help cover the bill.

Enter Barcelona

Word of Lionel's abilities reached a sports agent named Josep Maria Minguella. "I had a big network of scouts in South America and one of them told me there was a kid in Rosario who was only twelve but that he was unique," recalled Minguella. That kid was Lionel Messi.

One of the scouts sent a video of Lionel to Minguella. It showed Lionel playing keepie-uppies—first with an orange and then with a tennis ball. The video persuaded Minguella to contact a friend of his named Carles ("Charly") Rexach. Rexach worked as a scout for Fútbol Club (FC) Barcelona in Spain. Rexach had played for the club from 1965 to 1981 and won the Pichichi Trophy in 1971. (The Pichichi Trophy is awarded each year by a Spanish newspaper called

Opposite: Sixteen-year-old Lionel Messi wears his Barcelona uniform.

Marca to the player in the Spanish league who scores the most goals in a season.) More recently, Rexach had become a member of the club's coaching staff.

Rexach wasn't sold on the boy. He worried that Lionel was too young. Further, FC Barcelona rarely worked with children from outside Spain. Indeed, the club had never signed a boy Lionel's age from outside Spain or the European Union (EU). He told Minguella that the boy would have to be truly phenomenal for the club to take an interest in him. Minguella assured Rexach that Lionel was just what they needed.

Although Rexach was still doubtful, he invited Lionel to Barcelona for a two-week tryout. Lionel and Jorge arrived in Barcelona in September of 2000. The day after he arrived, Lionel suited up to practice with the FC Barcelona youth team. The other players eyed him with interest. "In the dressing room, they looked at him and could not believe how small he was," said soccer journalist Sid Lowe. However, "on the pitch, they looked at him and couldn't believe how good he was." One player named Marc Pedraza recalled, "The day when Messi arrived, and we saw how small he was, how skinny he was, we thought we were going to eat him. But when he touched the ball, we saw that he was a phenomenon. It was impossible to get the ball off him." Rexach agreed. "After two minutes, I knew," he said. "We have to sign this kid right now." Lionel was unlike any player they had ever seen.

Rexach saw in Lionel "a kid who was very small, but different, with incredible self-confidence, agile, fast, technically polished, who would run flat out with the ball, and who was capable of swerving round whoever stood in his way." Rexach continued, "It wasn't difficult to spot it; his talents, which are now known to everyone, were [even] more noticeable at thirteen." However, FC Barcelona didn't sign Lionel, at least not right away. Despite Rexach's confidence in Lionel, not everyone at the club thought signing a tiny thirteen-year-old boy with a medical condition was such a great idea. "Technically, nobody doubted him. He was unique," said Minguella. "But people said he would get slaughtered when other players tackled him. His problem was his physique." These doubters dragged their feet.

In December, Minguella and another sports agent named Horacio Gaggioli took Rexach to lunch and issued an ultimatum: Put a deal down in writing, or Lionel would go elsewhere. This was no idle threat. Other teams had expressed interest in the boy, including AC Milan, Real Madrid, and Atlético Madrid. Rexach did not want to let Lionel slip through the club's fingers. He wrote out a "contract" on the only paper available: a napkin. The contract read:

> In Barcelona on 14 December 2000 in the presence of Minguella and Horacio, Carles Rexach, technical director of FCB, commits to the signing, regardless of some opinions to the contrary of Lionel Messi, as long as the figures previously agreed are respected.

All three men signed the napkin. (Gaggioli still has it. He keeps it in a bank vault.) Jorge was satisfied, Lionel stayed with FC Barcelona, and the rest, as they say, is history. "No one wanted to take a risk with me," said Messi of the period before he signed with FC Barcelona. "It was a big gamble to sign such a small kid from abroad and bring him to Barcelona." He continued, "It was Charly Rexach who made it happen ... It was thanks to him and the coaches who wanted to sign me, although there were some who didn't!" This moment would change Lionel Messi's life forever.

Lionel Messi has practiced for long hours in the Barcelona training complex.

A Brief History of Spanish Soccer and FC Barcelona

When Lionel Messi tried out for FC Barcelona in September of 2000, the team was already more than one hundred years old. It was started by a twenty-two-year-old Swiss soccer champion named Hans Gamper. After moving from Switzerland to Barcelona in 1899, Gamper placed an advertisement in a local newspaper seeking fellow soccer enthusiasts to form a team. Ten players responded. The team met for the first time in November 1899. FC Barcelona was just one of several Spanish soccer clubs to start around this time. Others included Sevilla Fútbol Club (1890), Athletic Bilbao (1898), Espanyol (1900), Real Madrid (1902), Atlético Madrid (1903), and Real Sociedad (1909).

At first, FC Barcelona was an amateur club. It played most of its matches against similar teams in the region. In May 1902, FC Barcelona and four other Spanish soccer teams played in the first-ever national tournament. This knockout tournament was played to celebrate the coronation of Spanish king Alfonso XIII. It was called the Copa de Coronaçion. FC Barcelona made it to the final but lost to a team of top players from Bilbao. The tournament became an annual event and was renamed the Copa del Rey (King's Cup). It is still played today. FC Barcelona won its first Copa del Rey in 1910. As of 2019, it has won thirty.

In 1909, several top Spanish soccer teams, including FC Barcelona, joined together to form the Real Federación Española de Fútbol (RFEF). The RFEF has been soccer's governing body in Spain ever since. In 1913, the RFEF joined the Fédération Internationale de Football Association (FIFA), which was established in 1904.

FC Barcelona has a long and rich history.

In 1926, FC Barcelona became a professional team. Three years later, the RFEF started a professional championship league called La Liga. La Liga originally fielded ten teams including FC Barcelona. The league used a round-robin format to decide which team was champion. Each of the ten teams played every other team twice during the course of a La Liga season—once at home and once away—for a total of eighteen games. Teams were awarded three points for each win, one point for each tie, and zero points for each loss. Whichever team had the most points at the end of the season—which lasted from August to May—claimed the title. La Liga uses the same round-robin and points format today but fields twenty teams rather than ten. FC Barcelona won the first-ever La Liga tournament. As of 2019, it has won twenty-five.

In 1955, a new soccer federation formed called the Union of European Football Associations (UEFA). UEFA governed the various national football associations in Europe, including the RFEF. In 1956, UEFA organized a season-long tournament called the European Cup to allow the various European soccer clubs to establish an accurate hierarchy, or classification of teams based on professional standing. Later, the European Cup changed its name to Champions League. Sixteen teams played in the first European Cup championship, including FC Barcelona. The tournament became a yearly event. The field eventually expanded to thirty-two teams. FC Barcelona won its first UEFA title in 1992. It has won five as of 2019.

FC Barcelona is one of the world's most successful soccer teams, but it hasn't always been this way. The team's worst season was in 1941–1942. That year, it narrowly escaped relegation. Relegation is when a team in La Liga is demoted to the division below it (called La Liga 2). This happens at the end of each season to the three lowest-ranked teams in La Liga. Relegated teams are replaced by the top two clubs in La Liga 2 and the winner of a playoff game. FC Barcelona narrowly avoided this fate in the 1941–1942 season but hasn't come close since. FC Barcelona is one of just three original members of La Liga never to face relegation. (The other two are Real Madrid and Athletic Bilbao.)

For FC Barcelona fans, the team is more than a club. In fact, "*Més que un club*" ("More than a club") is the team's motto. The team is a symbol of Catalan culture, which was nearly extinguished during the Spanish Civil War (1936–1939) and the reign of General Francisco Franco (1939–1975). "Catalan" is a word used to describe people who live in Catalonia. Catalonia is the region of Spain in which Barcelona is located. In an attempt to unify Spain under his rule, Franco brutally oppressed the Catalan people, including members of FC Barcelona. (Franco preferred Real Madrid—just one reason for the intense rivalry between the two clubs.) FC Barcelona became a symbol of Catalan pride and of resistance against Franco.

Dealing with Red Tape

The famous napkin contract seemingly secured Lionel Messi's future with Barcelona, but Lionel still needed to sign a proper contract with the team. First, there were lots of details to work out: Who would pay for Lionel's medical treatment? (The team would pay for the treatment.) Where would he live? (He would live with his family in an apartment near the team's stadium.) Who would pay for the apartment? (The team would pay for the apartment.) Where would Lionel attend school? (He would attend a nearby school called León XIII—although he was admittedly not terribly fond of studying.) Where would Lionel's father work? (His father would work for a security firm owned by the team.) Would the team sign Lionel to its top squad when the time was right? (It would.) Finally, in March 2001, Lionel signed his first contract with Barcelona.

Lionel was officially a member of FC Barcelona and could enroll in the club's youth soccer academy. The academy is called La Masía (the Farmhouse) or La Cantera (the Quarry). Its purpose is to assemble top young athletes from Catalonia and other parts of Spain as well as the occasional international player like Lionel to train and play. Some players even live at the academy—although Lionel did not. Since it started in 1979, hundreds of players have trained at La Masía. Many have gone on to impressive soccer careers.

Now, Lionel faced a new problem: paperwork. Newell's Old Boys and the Argentine Football Association refused to process the paperwork needed for Lionel to transfer to FC Barcelona. That meant he was not free to play for the club in national or international competitions. He could play only in friendly games (matches between sports teams and especially international teams that have no connection with league or championship play) or in regional matches. FIFA got involved to settle the matter. In February 2002, it ruled in favor of Lionel and FC Barcelona. At last he was free to play full-time for his new team.

Working His Way Up the Ladder

As soon as Lionel became eligible to play full-time for the FC Barcelona youth squad, he quickly made his mark. In February 2002, during his first game on the national stage, he scored three goals after entering the game as a substitute in the second half. Lionel raced through the La Masía ladder system—from the Cadete squad, to Juvenil B, to Juvenil A, to Barcelona C, to Barcelona B—in just over eighteen months. Sometimes he played on multiple squads at the same time. In the Cadete category, said Messi, "we had a great team and the good fortune of winning everything … [we] didn't concede a single match." The team won its league as well as the Catalan and Spanish championships. The team became known as the Baby Dream Team.

The Baby Dream Team is still regarded as Barcelona's greatest-ever youth squad. Lionel was the top scorer on the Baby Dream Team with thirty-six goals in thirty games. "He was really good," said Gerard Piqué, who played alongside Messi on the Baby Dream Team. "But he was really small and thin … One coach said, 'Don't try to tackle him strong, because maybe you will break him.' And we said, 'OK, but don't worry because we cannot catch him.'" He is still regarded as one of the fastest players with the best dribbling skills.

Lionel's coaches were also impressed—and not just by his incredible skill. They liked his dedication. They appreciated how he gladly played for any squad—regardless of level. "You could say to him, 'Look here's the ball, let's play a match' and he would get on with it. He just loved playing. He didn't mind what level," said Albert Benaiges, who worked at La Masía. "Some kids when they play for the A team and then you ask them to play for the B team they pull a face but with him he always gave you everything." Coach Pere Gratacós was amazed by how Lionel could move from team to team—each with its own unique set of players and formations—and still deliver. The coaches were also moved by his class and generosity—the way he set up other players to score almost as often as he tried to score himself.

There was one other piece of good news during this period: Messi completed his medical treatments. He had grown to a height of 5 feet 7 inches (1.7 m) and a weight of 148 pounds (67 kilograms). He was well within normal range—although still on the small side.

Some people have accused Messi of gaining an unfair advantage from his growth hormone treatment. This is because adult athletes sometimes inject growth hormones to become bigger and stronger, which is against the rules in most sports. However, this criticism is unfounded. Dr. Diego Schwarzstein, who treated Messi in Rosario, explained, "You have to differentiate between growth hormone treatment for an adult who doesn't need it, who is looking for a physical benefit … and the treatment of a physical deficiency in a young boy." Soccer journalist Gavin Cooney likened Lionel's use of growth hormone to an asthmatic athlete using an inhaler.

Handling Homesickness and Overcoming Shyness

At first, the whole Messi family—Lionel, Jorge, Celia, Rodrigo, Matías, and María Sol—moved to Spain. However, María Sol struggled in school, and Rodrigo and Matías missed their friends

Gerard Piqué played alongside Lionel Messi on the Barcelona Baby Dream Team.

back home. In the summer of 2001, Lionel's mother and siblings moved back to Rosario. Jorge gave Lionel the opportunity to return home with them, but he refused. He knew that if he wanted to become a professional soccer player, he needed to stay in Barcelona.

It was Lionel's choice to stay in Barcelona, but it wasn't easy. "It was a complicated time," he said. "On the one hand, it was spectacular to come play at Barcelona. On the other, leaving everything behind in Rosario was tough: my friends, the rest of my family, my childhood." Lionel often shut himself in his room to cry so his father wouldn't see.

To make matters worse, Lionel was painfully shy. Making friends was hard—especially when bureaucratic matters prevented him from playing full-time. "We thought he was mute," said Gerard Piqué. "He said nothing to us for the first month." Another Baby Dream Team teammate named Víctor Vázquez recalled, "He would always return to the dressing room, sit down in a corner, change, and leave without a word." Then, said Piqué, "We traveled to Switzerland to play a tournament, and he started to talk and have fun. We thought it was another person." Diego Maradona didn't believe that Messi was shy and timid: "He's guarded with the press or people who don't know him. With his family or his friends, he's very amusing." It just took a little bit of time for some people to get to know Lionel.

A Series of Firsts

In November 2003, the coach of FC Barcelona's first team, Frank Rijkaard, had a problem. Several of his top players were injured. He needed some healthy athletes to fill his roster for an upcoming friendly game in Portugal against FC Porto. To fill in the gaps, Rijkaard promoted a few players from the FC Barcelona B squad to

Barcelona coach Frank Rijkaard gave Messi his first shot on the club's top squad.

the first team—including Lionel Messi. Lionel made his debut with the club's top squad on November 16, 2003. He was sixteen years old. "It was a very happy day," recalled Messi. "I was able to fulfill my childhood dream … when I got on I just enjoyed the moment." He had just one regret: He failed to score. "I had a really good chance against the goalkeeper, but I didn't get hold of it," he said. Moments like this were hard on Lionel because he was very competitive.

The first-team friendly in Porto was a one-off. As soon as it was over, Lionel returned to the Barcelona B squad—although he trained once a week with the A team. Lionel impressed the players on the top squad. One player whose name is Xavi recalled, "When I saw him in training, he was 16 years old, but [his talent] was already apparent … You already knew he was different. You could see he had innate quality going one-against-one, he was fast, he could score, he could shoot. It was something amazing." Another player, Ludovic Guily, agreed, "He destroyed us all. Every play he made was dangerous. It was incredible. He would dribble past four players and score a goal. He was an alien. He killed us all." After training with Lionel for the first time, the first team's star Ronaldo de Assis Moreira (commonly known as Ronaldinho) called a journalist friend. "I've just finished training with someone who is going to be better than me. He is so good," he said. Coaches and players started to see that Lionel would become a star on the pitch.

After practicing with Lionel for almost a year, players on the first team asked Rijkaard to promote him permanently. Rijkaard obliged. Once again, Lionel took to the field wearing a first-team jersey—this time as a substitute during a La Liga match against Espanyol on October 16, 2004.

At seventeen years, three months, and twenty-two days old, Lionel was the youngest athlete ever to represent Barcelona in an official competition. That season, he played eight more matches as a substitute on the club's first team while also playing as a starter on the Barcelona B squad.

Lionel scored his first-ever goal with the first team on May 1, 2005. He was the youngest Barcelona player ever to score a goal in official play. "My first goal was an indescribable feeling," said Messi. After stealing the ball from an opponent, Lionel passed it to Ronaldinho. Then, Ronaldinho chipped it back to Lionel. After faking a power shot, Lionel lobbed it over the goalkeeper. Ronaldinho then ran to Lionel to hug him. His teammates were ecstatic.

Success with Argentina's National Team

Although Lionel Messi had lived in Spain since he was thirteen years old (and would even claim Spanish citizenship in September 2005 to comply with certain La Liga rules), he considered himself Argentine. So, when the Argentine Football Association (AFA) invited Messi to join Argentina's junior national team for players under the age of twenty (U-20) in 2004, he happily accepted.

Messi played several games and tournaments with Argentina's U-20 squad. Despite being among the youngest players, he quickly became a leader on the team. His coaches and trainers were thrilled with his performance.

One coach named Hugo Tocalli recalled, "I loved his change of pace from zero to a hundred in no time at all, his trick of dodging past his opponent, his ability to move extremely fast with the ball

Lionel Messi celebrates winning the 2005 U-20 World Cup with the Argentine squad.

Messi versus Ronaldo

Some soccer fans say Lionel Messi is the greatest player of his generation—and maybe ever. Others say a different player has earned that title: a player from Portugal named Cristiano Ronaldo. Either way, both are incredibly talented soccer players.

Messi and Ronaldo are similar on the field. They've scored an almost identical number of goals in career

Messi's biggest rival is Cristiano Ronaldo.

league play as of summer 2019: Ronaldo with 597 and Messi with 591 (although Ronaldo has played many more matches than Messi). In addition, as of 2019, Messi has won more national league titles (nine) than Ronaldo (five), but Ronaldo has won more Champions League tournaments (five) than Messi (four).

Messi and Ronaldo have a lot in common off the field, too. Both had humble beginnings. (Ronaldo's mother was a cook, and his father was a gardener.) Both had medical problems as children. (Ronaldo had a heart condition that required surgery.) Both became professional soccer players at a young age. (Ronaldo quit school at the age of fourteen to focus entirely on soccer.) That's not to say everything about them is the same. They have different physiques. (Ronaldo is much larger.) They also have different personalities. (Ronaldo is showier and more temperamental.)

Even though the two men are undoubtedly rivals, they are not enemies. "We have always had a good relationship," Messi said. "We're colleagues, we just don't have daily contact because we play at different clubs. But there has always been respect and admiration on both sides." Because they both have a competitive nature, they use their rivalry to continue to push each other on the pitch.

still glued to his foot." In 2005, Argentina's U-20 squad was one of twenty-four teams to qualify for the FIFA U-20 World Cup in Holland.

Like the regular World Cup, the U-20 World Cup is played every four years. World Cup tournaments (including the U-20 World Cup) start with a type of round-robin phase called group play. In group play, there are six groups with four teams each. Each team in a group plays all the other teams in that group. Teams earn three points for each win, one point for each draw, and zero points for each loss. The two teams with the most points in each group—along with the four third-place finishers with the most points—advance to a knockout round of sixteen teams.

The Argentine team finished second in its group (after the United States but ahead of Egypt and Germany) to advance to the knockout round. The team then defeated Colombia, Spain, Brazil, and Nigeria to win the tournament.

Argentina's success at the U-20 World Cup was due in large part to Lionel Messi. He scored six goals during the tournament—more than any other player. For this, Messi won the Adidas Golden Boot award. Messi also won the Adidas Golden Ball award for being voted the top player in the tournament.

From Substitute to Starter

Lionel Messi made his debut first-team appearance for Barcelona in November 2003, but it wasn't until the 2005–2006 season that he was promoted to play on the club's top team full-time. Then, it wasn't until the 2006–2007 campaign that Messi became a regular starter on the pitch.

Messi quickly became an FC Barcelona fan favorite. He also caught the eye of soccer journalists. The Spanish media started calling him the "Messiah." After the 2007 season, he was voted the third-best player in all of Europe. He was just twenty years old.

As Messi's fortunes rose, FC Barcelona's fell. After winning the La Liga title in 2006, the team dropped to second in the standings in 2007 and third in 2008. They fared even worse in Champions League play. They won the Champions League in 2006 but failed to advance beyond the round of sixteen in 2007—although they did make it as far as the semifinals in 2008.

As for the Copa del Rey, the team hadn't won one of those since the 1990s. FC Barcelona would need to make some hard decisions in the months leading up to the 2008–2009 season. These decisions would have a huge impact on Messi.

FINAL LOND
28 MAIG-WEMB
FINAL 2011
FINAL 2011
UEFA
EUROPÉENS

Chapter 4

Lionel Rising

After two unsuccessful seasons, FC Barcelona decided to shake things up in 2008. The club released its coach (Frank Rijkaard) and star player (Ronaldinho). Messi signed a new contract that promised an annual salary of €7.8 million ($8.86 million). He was the highest-paid player on the team—and its new star player.

The Sextuple Season

The team's investment in Messi proved wise. During the 2008–2009 season, Messi scored thirty-eight goals in fifty-one games. He also led the team to the La Liga title, the Copa del Rey, and the Champions League championship—a feat called a continental treble. That wasn't all. FC Barcelona won the Supercopa de España (Spanish Super Cup)—a mini tournament that, as of 2018, is played by the winners and runners-up of La Liga and the Copa del Rey.

The team also won the European Super Cup. This is a match between the winner of the Champions League and the winner of the

Opposite: Lionel Messi celebrates Barcelona's victory in the Champions League tournament in 2011.

Barcelona star Lionel Messi outruns his opponents.

UEFA Europa League. (The Europa League is one level down from the Champions League.) The team also won the FIFA Club World Cup. This is a knockout tournament played by top club teams from around the world. Winning these six top-tier trophies in a single calendar year is called a sextuple. FC Barcelona is the only team ever to win a sextuple as of 2019.

In addition to winning a sextuple, FC Barcelona also won all three matches against its archrival Real Madrid. Games played between these two teams are called El Clásico. El Clásico is one of the greatest rivalries in sports. FC Barcelona and Real Madrid "hate each other with the bitter intensity of 1000 pickled lemons," explained sportswriter Dan Rookwood. Any win against Real Madrid—let alone three in a single season—is particularly sweet for FC Barcelona.

Messi notched another impressive victory during this period: an Olympic gold medal with Argentina's national team at the 2008 Beijing games. "The Olympic gold in 2008 is the win that I value the most because it is a tournament that you may only play once in your life," said Messi. In the final game, Messi proved essential to the team while assisting on the goal from Angel di Maria. He also put a lot of pressure on the defense. Argentina defeated Nigeria 1–0.

More Success

Messi and FC Barcelona very nearly scored an unprecedented second sextuple in the 2010–2011 season. They won La Liga, Champions League, the Supercopa de España, the European Super Cup, and the FIFA Club World Cup. Only the Copa del Rey eluded the team that year. (FC Barcelona lost to Real Madrid in the final by one goal.) A quintuple would have to do.

Messi became team captain of the Barcelona squad in 2018.

The team scored a second quintuple during the 2014–2015 season. That year, it was the Supercopa de España that got away. In the 2015–2016 and 2017–2018 seasons, the squad won a Spanish treble—a feat that involves winning La Liga, the Copa del Rey, and the Supercopa de España.

Of course, not every season was so successful. In 2009–2010 and 2012–2013, the team managed to win only La Liga and the Supercopa de España—still good but less than they'd hoped for. In 2011–2012 and 2016–2017, they won only the Copa del Rey. In 2013–2014, they failed to capture any titles at all.

Still, no one can dispute the overall success of FC Barcelona since Messi signed on. Since Messi became a regular on the club's first team, the squad has won eleven La Liga titles, six Copas del Rey, eight Supercopas de España, four Champions League titles, three UEFA Super Cups, and three FIFA Club World Cup titles as of 2019.

In May 2018, Messi became team captain of the FC Barcelona squad. Some have said he might not be suited for the role because of his quiet nature. One such person is Diego Maradona. "I love [Messi] with all my heart, he is a phenomenon, but they want to make him a leader, and he will never be a leader," Maradona commented. Others disagree, noting his leadership qualities—in particular, his humility, modesty, intensity, and passion. FC Barcelona's director of football, Eric Abidal, said, "He's an example as a captain. Not just talent-wise, also as a person ... We always say that Messi doesn't need to talk. Everyone knows when he's angry and everyone knows when he's happy." As for Messi, he's pleased to be captain. "It's a source of great pride to be captain. I know what it means to wear the armband," he said. Messi has even been characterized as one of soccer's greatest captains by ESPN.

Special Skills

Messi was a tiny boy—much smaller than his peers. Even after he reached his full height and weight after completing his medical treatments, he was still on the small side. However, being small gave Messi an edge on the pitch. "Small players have huge advantages over big players. They can start, stop and turn quicker. The best players are all small," explained former FC Barcelona coach Laureano Ruiz. Messi himself has said that being smaller makes him faster and more agile than bigger players and has enabled him to control the ball better.

When it comes to speed and agility—particularly with the ball at his feet—no one is better than Messi. He routinely blows by whole packs of players when the goal is in his sights. Indeed, his speed with the ball nearly matches his speed without it. When Messi dribbles, it's as if the ball is tied to his foot. He rarely loses control of the ball.

Another remarkable skill is his ability to stay on his feet. Hundreds of highlight clips show Messi bouncing like a pinball from defender to defender but never falling down. Experts attribute this to his low center of gravity—again, a product of his small size. When Messi does fall, he typically pops right back up. This is unusual in a sport "where players roll around on the ground like gunshot victims when an opponent so much as breathes on them," said journalist Wright Thompson. This is called diving. "Even as a kid I decided I would never be a diver on the field," said Messi. "If I can continue, I try to carry on, no matter what a defender does to attempt to

Quotes About Lionel

"He is the best player I have ever seen, and will ever see … He is a unique and irreplaceable footballer."

—Former FC Barcelona manager Pep Guardiola

"Messi is the Mozart of football."

—Football manager Radomir Antic

"I have seen the player who will inherit my place in Argentinian football and his name is Messi."

—Diego Maradona

"I like Messi a lot, he's a great player. Technically, we're practically at the same level."

—Brazilian retired football player Pelé

"Messi is the best player ever. And this is said by someone who has seen Maradona and Pelé play."

—Football manager Adriano Galliani

"It is clear that Messi is on a level above all others. Those who do not see that are blind."

—Former FC Barcelona teammate Xavi

"Messi has a divine gift."
—Former FC Barcelona teammate Dani Alves

"Messi is God, as a person and even more as a player. I knew him when he was a boy and I've watched him grow. He deserves it all."
—Former FC Barcelona teammate Samuel Eto'o

"He does not really seem human to me."
—Former FC Barcelona teammate Luis Enrique

"Both of us have a creative style of play. I try to do nice things with my hands, to be creative like Messi. I love watching him play."
—American basketball player Steph Curry

"I wear the number 10 Jersey for the US National Team in honor of the greatest athlete I have ever seen: Messi."
—Retired American basketball player Kobe Bryant

stop me." Since diving sometimes leads a player to gain an unfair advantage, it is very controversial in soccer.

Often, the only way to stop Messi is to foul him, which happens a lot. In one rough installment of the El Clásico rivalry, Real Madrid's strategy was "to use nasty muscle against Messi, to shoulder him down or shiver him with a forearm or take his legs in scything tackles," said Jeré Longman of the *New York Times*. Officials ignored many of these attacks. Messi "made small appeals for fairness with his eyes and hands, but he remained unflappable and without complaint," explained Longman. In a sport where diving is common, Messi's lack of dramatic actions is somewhat unique.

Messi never stops working on improving his game. "I've always wanted to improve, it's still one of my greatest motivations," Messi said. However, Messi's real talent is the joy he takes in playing. "He's still the boy who made the goals-for-cookies deal," said journalist Jeff Himmelman. "He plays like a boy: instinctive, free." Messi agrees. "I have fun like a child in the street. When the day comes when I'm not enjoying it, I will leave football." This love for the game, rather than the money, is why Messi is admired by so many soccer fans around the world.

Top Barcelona Teammates

Messi has played a huge part in the success of FC Barcelona. However, if you ask him about it, he often credits his teammates more than himself. "I'm lucky to be part of a team who help to make me look good, and they deserve as much of the credit for my success as I do for the hard work we have all put in on the training ground," Messi has said. "I have the best players in the world in

their positions around me and I'm on the best team in the world."
One teammate who had a particularly positive impact on Messi was Brazilian player Ronaldinho. He played for FC Barcelona from 2003 to 2008. Ronaldinho helped Messi adjust when he was promoted to the club's first team. "Dinho was our leader, the best player in the squad, and I learned a lot of things from him," said Messi. Messi even believes that Ronaldinho was a better player than he is. "I don't consider myself the greatest player in Barcelona's history. Because I know it's Ronaldinho." Messi's humility comes through when he acknowledges the skills of other players and tries to learn from them.

Spanish player Xavier Hernández Creus (known as Xavi) was another teammate who made a big difference for Messi. Xavi played alongside Messi from the time he joined the team until 2015. As far as Messi is concerned, Xavi is the best Spanish player of all time.

Another Spanish player named Andrés Iniesta shared the field with Messi from 2001 (on the Barcelona B squad) until 2018. "The hardest thing to do in football is to make it look like everything is easy, effortless, and that's Andrés," said Messi of Iniesta. "On the pitch, I like him to be near me, especially when the game takes a turn for the worse, when things are difficult."

A Brazilian player named Dani Alves was a teammate of Lionel Messi's from 2008 to 2016. The two of them are particularly close friends. "We've spent many years together, both on and off the field. Day-to-day, we've got a very strong relationship, which is also of a great help on the field—it means we understand each other's games very well," said Messi of Alves. More recently, Messi teamed up with two younger stars: a Brazilian named Neymar and a Uruguayan named Luis Suárez. Together the threesome—nicknamed MSN—scored an amazing 364 goals and racked up an incredible 173 assists between 2014 and 2017. "It's wonderful playing with them," Messi

FIFA
CLUB WORLD CUP

Lionel Messi (*left*) is shown here with Neymar (*center*) and Luis Suárez (*right*) following their FIFA Club World Cup win in 2015.

has said. "We get along really well on and off the pitch. We really are friends and that is really important to enable us to play this kind of football." Together, this threesome made history until Neymar left Barcelona for Paris Saint-Germain in 2017.

Dealing with Injury

Like many professional athletes, Messi has dealt with his share of injuries. Many of these have been minor—muscle strains that have resulted in a few weeks at most on the bench. Others have been more serious. A hamstring injury in March 2006 put Messi out of the rotation for seventy days. He sat out for an additional eighty-seven days with a broken foot in November of that same year. A knee injury in September 2015 took fifty-one days to heal.

Between April 2008 and April 2013, Messi sustained just one injury: a stretched ligament in September 2010 that put him out of rotation for seven days. Then, he suffered six injuries in succession—three hamstring injuries, two thigh injuries, and a torn muscle bundle—resulting in 126 days off the pitch.

In March 2014, Messi vomited on the pitch during a friendly game between the Argentine national team and the Romanian squad. It wasn't the first time. The same thing had happened in August 2011 and March 2013. Messi's diet was the problem. Messi has a weakness for pizza and soda. He also has a sweet tooth. The boy who had once swapped goals for alfajores had grown up to be a man who loved chocolate and desserts. Messi's diet was so poor that one FC Barcelona coach ordered the removal of a soda machine near the team's locker room to keep Messi from constantly gulping down the fizzy drinks.

Finally, Messi decided to change his diet. "What you can put into your body at eighteen or nineteen years of age is not the same as what you can put in at twenty-seven," Messi said. He started working with a nutritionist and replaced foods like cookies with healthier fare—things like whole grains, fresh fruit and vegetables, nuts, seeds, and fish. He also cut down on sugar and foods made from flour, such as bread. Since changing his diet, Messi no longer gets sick on the field, and he's fitter than ever.

Disappointment on the National Squad

When Messi was just eighteen years old, he led Argentina's U-20 squad to victory in the 2005 U-20 World Cup. Less than two months later, he made his debut on the senior Argentine squad. Sadly, Messi's record with La Albiceleste has been less than stellar—especially in World Cup play. (La Albiceleste is a nickname for the Argentine national team. It translates to "white and sky blue"—the colors on the team's striped jerseys.)

Messi played in his first World Cup tournament in 2006. Messi's playing time was limited due to the fact that he was one of the youngest athletes on the team. Perhaps because the Argentine coach declined to play Messi more often, La Albiceleste was eliminated by Germany in the quarterfinals.

Things went even worse for the team in 2010. First, the Argentine squad nearly failed to qualify for the World Cup at all. Then, history repeated itself when Germany eliminated the Argentines 4–0 in the quarterfinals. This time Messi—who served as team captain—had played considerable minutes. He therefore faced considerable criticism for his failure to lead the Argentine team to victory.

A dejected Messi (wearing the number 10 jersey) is shown here following Argentina's defeat by France in the 2018 World Cup round of 16. France went on to win the tournament.

In 2014, Messi and the team fared better. Messi scored seven goals in seven matches to lead the team to the World Cup final. Their opponent was Germany—again! During the game, Argentina took ten shots, but none of them found the net. Germany won the match 1–0 in extra time. Messi did win the Golden Ball trophy—awarded to the tournament MVP. That achievement meant little to Messi. "I don't care about the Golden Ball," Messi said at the time. "I wanted to lift the World Cup." Messi constantly pushes himself to achieve more and more in the game of soccer.

However, it wasn't just a World Cup title that eluded Messi. He also failed to capture another important title: the Copa América. The Copa América tournament is played every four years to decide the top national team in South America. Twice, Messi has led the Argentine squad to the finals (in 2007 and 2015), and twice, the squad has lost. The team also lost the final in the Copa América Centenaro—played in 2016 to commemorate the tournament's hundredth anniversary—in part because Messi missed a crucial penalty kick.

The 2016 Copa América Centenaro proved particularly painful for Messi—so much so that he announced his retirement from the Argentine squad:

> For me, the national team is over. I've done all I can. It hurts not to be a champion. It's been four finals. I tried. It was the thing I wanted the most, but I couldn't get it, so I think it's over. I think this is best for everyone. First of all for me, then for everyone … It's very hard, but the decision is taken.

Messi's retirement didn't stick. Tens of thousands of Argentine fans begged him to reconsider. Some even marched in the streets.

Messi then reversed his decision. "A lot of things went through my mind on the night of the final and I gave serious thought to quitting, but my love for my country and this shirt is too great," Messi said.

Messi still has not won a major tournament with the Argentine squad as of 2019. Indeed, the squad has not won a major title of any kind since 1993. The team lost to France in the round of 16 in the 2018 World Cup. (France went on to win the title.) However, Messi will no doubt keep trying. "I would trade all my personal achievements just to win the World Cup with the national team," Messi said. Messi will have his next—and perhaps last—opportunity in 2022 in Qatar.

EVE
Lionel Andrés Messi
Lionel Andrés Messi
Lionel Andrés Messi

Chapter 5

Lionel's Legacy

Lionel Messi is widely viewed as one of the greatest to ever play the game of soccer. This is for good reason. As of 2019, Messi has been the top scorer in La Liga play for five separate seasons: 2009–2010, 2011–2012, 2012–2013, 2016–2017, and 2017–2018. Messi has enjoyed similar success in Champions League play. He was the league's top scorer for four straight seasons from 2008–2009 to 2011–2012 and a fifth in 2014–2015. He is currently the all-time career top scorer in both leagues. He has also scored the most goals of any player in a single club season (73 in 2011–2012) and in a calendar year (91 in 2012), and he has completed more hat tricks than any other player (51) as of 2019.

Messi doesn't just score goals, though. He also creates opportunities for other players to score. These are called assists. A reporter once asked Messi if he preferred to score or to set someone else up for a goal. "It's the same," Messi replied with a shrug. Messi holds the all-time career record for the number of assists in La Liga as of 2019.

Opposite: Messi is among the most decorated soccer players ever.

Awards Galore

Since 1956, *France Football* has honored the top player in Europe each year with a trophy called the Ballon d'Or (Golden Ball). The winner is selected based on a vote by soccer journalists. After finishing third in the voting in 2007 and second in 2008, Messi won the award for the first time in January 2009. Messi went on to win the Ballon d'Or four more times as of 2019: in 2010, 2011, 2012, and 2015. Only Cristiano Ronaldo has won as many Ballon d'Or awards as Messi. No one has won more.

Messi is also a six-time winner of the European Golden Shoe or Golden Boot award. This award goes to the player who scores the most goals in European league competition. Messi won this award in 2010, 2012, 2013, 2017, 2018, and 2019. He holds the record for the most Golden Shoes. He also holds the record for the most Best Player in La Liga awards (seven) and the most Best Forward in La Liga awards (eight). Messi is no doubt honored by this recognition, but in the end, "I don't care about personal awards," he said. "What I care about is to keep winning with my club and Argentina." Messi has a special place in his heart for Argentina.

Not Motivated by Money

During his time with FC Barcelona, Messi has become one of the most accomplished, most famous, and wealthiest athletes in the world. According to a 2018 article in *Forbes*, Messi earned $84 million in salary and bonuses that year. He also earned an additional $27 million in endorsements from companies like Adidas, PepsiCo, Gillette, Dolce & Gabbana, Turkish Airlines, EA Sports, and others. He was the second highest paid athlete in the world that

Career Highlights

Lionel Messi's career has many highlights—so many, in fact, it's hard to decide which ones to mention. One early and obvious highlight was winning the 2005 U-20 World Cup with the Argentine junior national team. Messi later called this "one of the biggest achievements of my career." A highlight with the Argentine senior squad was winning the Olympic gold medal in Beijing in 2008.

Messi's first-ever goal with Barcelona in 2005 was a major career highlight. Another highlight was winning six major championships in a single season in 2008–2009: La Liga, Copa del Rey, Champions League, Supercopa de España, European Super Cup, and FIFA Club World Cup (a feat known as the sextuple). The same season, Messi also led FC Barcelona to victory in all three El Clásico matches against Real Madrid—yet another highlight. (Speaking of El Clásico, Messi holds the record for the all-time number of goals scored in this series.) During the 2012–2013 season, Messi logged the longest goal-scoring run in La Liga history. He scored at least one goal in ten consecutive games—thirty-three in all. This record remains unbroken.

Even though Messi does not focus much on personal awards, winning his first Ballon d'Or in 2009—the first of five—was a big moment. It was also a big moment when he won his first European Golden Shoe award in 2010—again, the first of six. More recently, Messi became team captain of FC Barcelona—an honor of which he is very proud.

year (after boxer Floyd Mayweather). The next year, he became the world's highest paid athlete!

Despite his status and wealth, Messi is not motivated by money. He said, "Money doesn't thrill me or make me play better because there are benefits to being wealthy. I'm just happy with a ball at my feet. My motivation comes from playing the game I love. If I wasn't paid to be a professional footballer I would willingly play for nothing." While it's often hard to stay humble with Messi's kind of wealth, he manages to do so.

Between 2007 and 2009, Messi's disinterest in finances had negative consequences. According to Spanish authorities, he failed to pay more than €4.1 million ($4.6 million) in taxes. When Messi —who relied on his father and advisors to handle his financial affairs—found out about this lapse, he paid back the taxes plus a €2.8 million ($3.1 million) fine.

Messi claimed he was not aware of the terms laid out in the various legal and financial documents his advisors asked him to sign. "I was playing football. I had no idea about anything," he told the court. Jorge Messi lodged a similar defense. "All of this was like basic Chinese to me, I did not understand anything," he said. "I asked [the advisors] to look after our assets ... They told us this was the best way." Despite these arguments, Spanish authorities convicted Messi and his father of tax fraud.

The court ruled that Messi was ultimately responsible for his finances even if he let other people handle them. The court also argued that while Messi might not have been aware of the fraud, he had benefited from it nonetheless. Both Lionel and Jorge Messi were sentenced to twenty-one months in prison, but neither was required to serve jail time because this was a first offense.

Life Off the Pitch

Messi spends hours each day on the pitch. Off the pitch, he spends most of his free time at home with his family. Lionel's life partner is a fellow Rosarian named Antonella Roccuzzo. He has known her since he was just nine years old. She is the cousin of one of Lionel's closest childhood friends. Her father owned a chain of supermarkets in Rosario. "Lionel has always liked Antonella, since forever," recalled a longtime friend of Lionel's. "Every time Messi saw her, he blushed." For Lionel, it was love at first sight.

When Lionel left Rosario for Barcelona, the two lost touch. They reconnected sometime around 2007 and went public with their romance in 2009—the same year Lionel completed the sextuplet with Barcelona. In 2010, Antonella moved to Barcelona to live with Lionel. Friends say they are the love of each other's lives.

Antonella—whom Lionel often calls Anto—has worked as a model, but she is quite down to earth. She studied dentistry and then communications in school. Not content to rely on Lionel for her income, she partnered with the wife of one of Lionel's teammates to open a luxury shoe shop in Barcelona in 2017.

In 2012, Antonella gave birth to the couple's first child—a son, named Thiago. Two more sons followed: Mateo in 2015 and Ciro in 2018. Lionel was present for all three births. Lionel loves being a dad. "Being a father has helped me grow up. It has helped me to stop being so obsessed over football and to realize that there are other things in life too," he said. "I'm ecstatic about the family we have been able to create." Family is very important to Lionel.

On June 30, 2017, Lionel and Antonella got married at a luxury hotel in Rosario. The Argentine press dubbed the event the

The Messi family is pictured here in 2017 (*from left to right*): Antonella, Mateo, Lionel, and Thiago. A third son, Ciro, arrived in 2018.

"wedding of the century." The two exchanged vows in front of some 260 guests. These included many of Messi's current and former teammates such as Luis Suárez, Neymar, and Gerard Piqué. Also present was the pop star Shakira, who is Piqué's partner.

The Messi family leads a remarkably simple life. "It's a normal, calm life, the kind of life we have always wanted," Messi said. A typical day for Messi involves dropping his older boys off at school, training with the team, and hanging out at home and drinking tea or visiting a local park.

They might lead a simple life—but it's still a life of luxury. They live in a modern-style mansion in the ritzy village of Castelldefels just outside Barcelona. The property—which overlooks both the Catalan mountains and the Mediterranean Sea—boasts a private theater, a gym, a spa, and a swimming pool. The property even has a soccer pitch where Lionel often practices or plays with his two dogs.

The property also features a large garage—a requirement for storing Messi's impressive collection of expensive cars. These include a Ferrari F430 Spider, a Maserati GranTurismo MC Stradale, and an Audi R8 Spyder. Messi also owns a 1957 Ferrari 335 Sport Spider Scaglietti—a classic car bought at auction for €32 million ($37 million). It is said to be the most expensive car ever. However, even though Messi owns many nice things, he still believes his children and family are the most important part of his life, and he enjoys spending time with them above all else.

Messi remains close with his parents and siblings and with a few friends back in Rosario. However, apart from a few FC Barcelona teammates, Messi "hasn't made a new friend in a long time," said journalist Wright Thompson. "Most of his confidants were teammates on the Machine of '87." In fact, speaking of Rosario,

Messi has made Barcelona his home. He lives there with his family in a modern-style mansion with a view of the Catalan mountains and the Mediterranean Sea.

Messi has lived in Barcelona for longer than he ever lived in Rosario. However, he has never lost his Argentine accent. "Messi has retained it all his life," said Jeff Himmelman of the *New York Times*. "I have my feet firmly on the ground and I never forget where I came from," said Messi. Even though Messi is now rich and famous, he is still himself. However, he has changed in one important way—he's less shy. "When he debuted, he was a very well-balanced person, calm, respectful, and very shy," said Frank Rijkaard. "Over time, he has changed a lot, but without losing these attributes. Now he is more sure of himself ... he is not the silent boy he was all those years ago. He is funnier, he likes to joke around when he is with his teammates or surrounded by people he knows." Some might say that Messi found his confidence and sense of self on the pitch.

Charitable Work

Messi knows how fortunate he has been in his life both on and off the field. To share his good fortune, he works closely with several charities. He is particularly interested in charities that help children—especially kids who suffer from health ailments.

One of these charities is the United Nations Children's Fund (UNICEF). Messi has volunteered for UNICEF since 2004. He has participated in many UNICEF campaigns to draw attention to important issues concerning children. One of these focused on promoting the social inclusion of children who suffer from disabilities. Another important issue was to push for HIV prevention. A third one highlighted the high mortality rates among disadvantaged children. In that campaign, Messi was joined by his son Thiago.

In 2007, Messi visited a hospital for terminally ill children. He was so moved by the children he met that he created his own charitable organization called the Lionel Messi Foundation. The focus of this foundation is to support children's access to health care, education, and sports.

The Lionel Messi Foundation frequently partners with UNICEF to fund important projects for children. One recent project was the installation of twenty classrooms for children in Syria. Perhaps a more personal project was the construction of a new gymnasium and dormitory for the youth academy at his old club in Rosario, Newell's Old Boys. Through the foundation, Messi has also donated money to his old school for the construction of a new playground and other facilities.

Lionel Messi is shown here with Afghan boy Murtaza Ahmadi on the pitch before the start of a friendly match against Saudi Arabia's Al-Ahli FC on December 13, 2016.

Messi is generous in other ways, too. For their wedding, Lionel and Antonella asked their wedding guests to donate to Lionel's charity instead of buying the couple gifts. Then, they donated all the leftover food and drinks from the event to a local food bank.

Even more moving was when Messi spotted a photograph of a five-year-old boy in Afghanistan named Murtaza Ahmadi kicking a ball in the dirt. The boy was wearing a sky-blue-and-white striped plastic bag with "Messi" and the number 10 scrawled on it. Messi sent the boy a signed Albiceleste jersey and even flew him to a game in Qatar so he could meet him in person.

During matches, Messi sometimes wears special undershirts with the name of a charity or medical condition. Then, when he scores a goal, he lifts up his jersey to show the undershirt to the cameras. An image of the shirt is then beamed around the world.

This act raises awareness of the charity or condition. For example, in 2009, Messi wore an undershirt with the words "Síndrome X Frágil" (Fragile X syndrome), which is a genetic disorder that causes intellectual disabilities. Messi's support of Fragile X patients both on and off the pitch has been very meaningful.

What's Next?

Most likely, Lionel Messi will continue to play professional soccer for many more years. The question is, where? He has given some clues. "I'm increasingly sure that in Europe, Barcelona will be my only club," Messi told a reporter in 2018. "I'm not tempted to leave Barça," Messi has said. "There is nowhere better than Barça. If I wasn't here I wouldn't be anywhere. It's the best team in the world, the best city in the world ... I do not need to go anywhere else to prove anything." Messi has always been very successful with Barcelona, but he has been unable to fulfill his potential in that same way elsewhere.

Recently, Messi has also begun talking about potentially moving back to Rosario to play for his old club, Newell's Old Boys. "I always said I wanted to play in Argentine football one day," Messi commented. "I don't know if it will happen but I have it in my mind. It would be at Newell's, nowhere else." Messi has achieved almost everything possible on the pitch. Only a World Cup title has eluded him (at least for now). Messi explained, "I'm more worried about being a good person than being the best football player in the world. When this is all over, what are you left with? When I retire, I hope I am remembered for being a decent guy." Lionel Messi is more than just a great soccer player—he is a role model for people around the world.

Timeline

June 24, 1987 Lionel Messi is born in Rosario, Argentina.

2001 Messi officially joins FC Barcelona as a junior player.

2003 Messi plays his first-ever match with the FC Barcelona first team, in a friendly against FC Porto in Portugal.

2004 Messi plays his first-ever match with the FC Barcelona first squad in official competition. He is the youngest player ever to do so.

2004–2005 Messi wins his first La Liga title.

2005 Messi scores his first-ever goal for the FC Barcelona first team. He leads the Argentine national U-20 team to a World Cup title.

2006 Messi wins his first Champions League title.

2008 Messi wins an Olympic gold medal with the Argentine national team.

2008–2009 Messi wins his first Copa del Rey. He leads FC Barcelona to a continental treble and the first-ever sextuple. Messi is also named La Liga Best Player and La Liga Best Forward for the first time.

2009 Messi wins the Ballon d'Or for the first time. He is named FIFA World Player of the Year.

2009–2010 Messi is the top scorer in La Liga for the first time.

2010 Messi wins the European Golden Shoe award for the first time.

2011–2012 Messi scores the most goals of any player in a single club season ever.

2012 Messi scores the most goals in a calendar year of any player ever.

2014 Messi leads the Argentine national team to the World Cup final. Argentina loses to Germany, but Messi wins the Golden Ball award.

2015 Messi is named World Soccer Player of the Year and GSA (Globe Soccer Awards) Best Player of the Year.

2016 Messi scores his fifty-fifth international goal during the Copa América Centenario tournament, breaking Gabriel Batistuta's Argentine score record.

2018 Messi becomes team captain of the FC Barcelona squad.

Glossary

assist The act of passing the ball to another player, giving him or her the opportunity to score.

association football A ball game played by two teams on a rectangular pitch with a goal on each end. The object of the game is to place the ball in the other team's goal. Players may not touch the ball with their hands or arms (except for the goalkeeper). This game is more commonly called football or soccer.

coup d'état An event in which a person or group seizes governmental power.

defender A player on a soccer team who plays closest to his or her team's goal. Defenders help the goalkeeper protect the goal.

diving The act of purposely falling to the ground after minor contact during play and pretending to be injured in an attempt to persuade the officials to call a foul on the opposing player.

draw Another word for tie.

dribble The act of moving the ball forward with repeated light kicks.

endocrinologist A doctor who specializes in health issues related to hormones.

forward A player on a soccer team who plays closest to the other team's goal. Forwards generally score more goals than players in other positions.

goalkeeper The player on a soccer team who protects the team's goal. Another word for goalkeeper is goalie.

hat trick A phrase describing when a single player scores three goals in one game.

hormones Chemicals in the body that control certain bodily functions such as growth.

keepie-uppies A game that involves using one's feet, knees, legs, chest, shoulders, or head to keep a ball or other object off the ground. Also called juggling.

knockout tournament A tournament format in which the winner of the match advances to the next round and the loser is eliminated.

La Albiceleste A nickname for the Argentine national team. It means "white and sky blue," which describes the team's jerseys.

match A soccer game.

midfielder A player on a soccer team who plays in the middle of the field, between the team's forwards and defenders.

nutmeg To kick the ball through a defending player's legs.

penalty kick A shot on goal taken by a player with only the opposing team's goalie to defend it.

pitch The field on which a soccer match is played.

quarterfinal A game or round in a tournament immediately before the semifinal round. The winner of a quarterfinal goes on to play in a semifinal.

relegation The demotion of a soccer club from one tier in a club's league to the tier below it.

round-robin A tournament format in which every competitor plays every other competitor at least once.

semifinal A game or round in a tournament immediately before the final. The winner of a semifinal goes on to play in the final.

shootout A period in a soccer game during which both teams take five penalty kicks. Whichever team scores the most goals during the shootout wins the game. Shootouts occur only in knockout tournaments if a game is tied after extra time.

treble An accomplishment in soccer that happens when a club team wins three trophies in a single season.

Further Information

Books

Balagué, Guillem. *Barca: The Illustrated History of FC Barcelona.* London, UK: Carlton Books, 2018.

Caioli, Luca. *Messi: More Than a Superstar.* London, UK: Icon Books, 2018.

Perez, Mike. *Lionel Messi: The Ultimate Fan Book.* London, UK: Carlton Books, 2017.

Savage, Jeff. *FC Barcelona: Soccer Champions.* Minneapolis, MN: Learner Publishing Group, 2018.

Shetty, Sanjeev. *Messigraphica: A Graphic Biography of the Genius of Lionel Messi.* London, UK: Aurum Press, 2017.

Websites

Champions League

https://www.uefa.com/uefachampionsleague/index.html
Keep up with Champions League action here.

ESPN FC: Lionel Messi

http://www.espnfc.com/player/45843/lionel-messi
This ESPN webpage features a profile of Lionel Messi, including statistics and career highlights.

FC Barcelona

https://www.fcbarcelona.com/en/
The official English-language website for FC Barcelona features schedules and results as well as information on players.

La Liga

https://www.laliga.es/en
This is the official English-language website for La Liga, featuring schedules, statistics, news, and more.

Lionel Messi's Official Website

https://messi.com
This official website for Lionel Messi includes news, statistics, information about his next matches, and much more.

Videos

Favorite Memories

https://www.fcbarcelona.com/en/videos/752905/leo-messi-shares-his-favourite-memories-with-beko
In this video with English subtitles, Lionel Messi describes his first soccer club, Grandoli.

Lionel Messi: Best Solo Goals

https://www.youtube.com/watch?v=MEWSjzw2jVw
This video shows a compilation of dozens of goals scored by Lionel Messi.

Bibliography

Balagué, Guillem. *Messi.* London, UK: Orion Publishing Group, 2013.

Borden, Sam. "Germans End Long Wait: 24 Years and a Bit Extra." *New York Times*, July 13, 2014. https://www.nytimes.com/2014/07/14/sports/worldcup/world-cup-2014-germany-defeats-argentina-in-final.html.

Burns, Jimmy. *Barca: A People's Passion.* London, UK: Bloomsbury Publishing, 2009.

Burnton, Simon. "Childhood Move to Barcelona Was Medicine for Lionel Messi." *Guardian*, April 20, 2010. https://www.theguardian.com/football/2010/apr/20/childhood-barcelona-medicine-lionel-messi.

Caioli, Luca. *Messi.* London, UK: Icon Books Limited, 2017.

Carlin, John. "Lionel Messi: Magic in His Feet." *Independent*, March 27, 2010. https://www.independent.co.uk/news/people/profiles/lionel-messi-magic-in-his-feet-1928768.html.

Carter, Chris. "Lionel Messi: The World's Most Expensive Football Player Who'd Play for Nothing." *Money Week*, July 1, 2015. https://moneyweek.com/372024/lionel-messi-the-worlds-most-expensive-football-player-whod-play-for-nothing/.

Domin, Martin. "How Barcelona Signed Leo Messi and Put Him on the Road to Greatness." *Mirror*, November 9, 2018. https://www.mirror.co.uk/sport/football/news/how-barcelona-signed-lionel-messi-13560602.

Faccio, Leonardo. *Messi: A Biography.* New York, NY: Anchor Sports, 2012.

Fitzpatrick, Richard. "Capturing the Atomic Flea: Inside the Deal That Took Lionel Messi to Barcelona." Bleacher Report, February 11, 2016. https://thelab.bleacherreport.com/capturing-the-atomic-flea/.

Fitzpatrick, Richard. "The Machine of '87: Messi's Boyhood Teammates Recall Early Signs of Greatness." Bleacher Report, June 23, 2017. https://bleacherreport.com/articles/2717227-the-machine-of-87-messis-boyhood-teammates-recall-early-signs-of-greatness.

Gupta, Shreya. "FIFA 2018: Inside Lionel Messi's $7 Million Mediterranean-Themed Barcelona Home." *Architectural Digest,* June 8, 2018. https://www.architecturaldigest.in/content/fifa-2018-lionel-messi-barcelona-home/.

Hanagudu, Ashwin. "Lionel Messi's 5 Favourite Teammates." Sportskeeda. Accessed on March 21, 2019. https://www.sportskeeda.com/football/lionel-messi-five-favourite-teammates.

Harvey, Joel. "The Dirty World Cup: Looking Back at Argentina '78." Versed, October 10, 2017. https://www.theversed.com/76555/the-dirty-world-cup-looking-back-at-argentina-78/#.X87rzqDv7x.

Hayward, Ben. "The Making of Lionel Messi: How It All Started for the Champions League's All-Time Top Goal Scorer." Goal.com. Accessed on March 2, 2019. https://www.goal.com/en-us/news/174/uefa-champions-league/2014/11/25/5331521/the-making-of-lionel-messi-how-it-all-started-for-the.

Himmelman, Jeff. "The Burden of Being Messi." *New York Times,* June 5, 2014. https://www.nytimes.com/2014/06/08/magazine/the-burden-of-being-messi.html.

Longman, Jeré. "Lionel Messi: Boy Genius." *New York Times,* May 21, 2011. https://www.nytimes.com/2011/05/22/sports/soccer/lionel-messi-boy-genius.html.

Lowe, Sid. "Lionel Messi: How Argentinian Teenager Signed for Barcelona on a Serviette." *Guardian,* October 15, 2014. https://www.theguardian.com/football/blog/2014/oct/15/lionel-messi-barcelona-decade.

Mehrotra, Aakriti. "Fascism & Football: The Political History of Spanish Football." Outside of the Boot. Accessed on March 17, 2019. http://outsideoftheboot.com/2014/05/22/fascism-football-the-political-history-of-spanish-football/.

Pathak, Rahul. "Lionel Messi's First Football Club." Al Jazeera, July 7, 2011. https://www.aljazeera.com/blogs/americas/2011/07/49961.html.

Perez, Mike. *Lionel Messi: The Ultimate Fan Book.* London, UK: Carlton Books, 2017.

Piette, Candace. "Argentine Home City's Pride in Football Star Messi." BBC, June 4, 2010. https://www.bbc.com/news/10207981.

Ritter, Karl. "Five Reasons Why Messi Stands Out in Soccer World." *Boston Globe,* July 12, 2014. https://www.bostonglobe.com/sports/2014/07/12/reasons-why-messi-stands-out-football-world/mreF1boxmpDQcq7ZWenjqJ/story.html.

Savage, Jeff. *FC Barcelona: Soccer Champions*. Minneapolis, MN: Learner Publishing Group, 2018.

Storey, Daniel. "Portrait of an Icon: Lionel Messi." Football365, January 4, 2017. https://www.football365.com/news/portrait-of-an-icon-lionel-messi.

Thompson, Wright. "Here & Gone: The Strange Relationship Between Lionel Messi and His Hometown in Argentina." ESPN. Accessed on March 19, 2019. http://www.espn.com/espn/eticket/story?page=lionel-messi.

Zahn, Max. "Lionel Messi Is the Highest Paid Soccer Player in the World. Here's How He Makes and Spends His Millions." Money.com, June 18, 2018. http://money.com/money/5313998/lionel-messi-net-worth/.

Index

Page numbers in **boldface** are images.

About the Author

Kate Shoup has written more than forty books and has edited hundreds more. When not working, Shoup loves to travel, watch IndyCar racing, ski, read, and ride her motorcycle. She lives in Indianapolis with her husband and their dog.